BECOMING FLAME

Becoming Flame

Uncommon

Mother-Daughter

Wisdom

ISABEL ANDERS

WIPF & STOCK · Eugene, Oregon

BECOMING FLAME
Uncommon Mother-Daughter Wisdom

Copyright © 2010 Isabel Anders. All rights reserved. Except for brief quotations in critical publications or reviews, no part of this book may be reproduced in any manner without prior written permission from the publisher. Write: Permissions, Wipf & Stock, 199 W. 8th Ave., Suite 3, Eugene, OR 97401.

Wipf & Stock
An Imprint of Wipf and Stock Publishers
199 W. 8th Ave., Suite 3
Eugene, OR 97401

www.wipfandstock.com

ISBN: 978-1-60899-266-9

Manufactured in the U.S.A.

Excerpt from Rejoice, Beloved Woman by Barbara J. Monda. Copyright © 2004. Used with permission of the publisher, Sorin Books, an imprint of Ave Maria Press ®, Inc., Notre Dame, Indiana 46556. www.avemariapress.com

New Revised Standard Version Bible, copyright © 1989, Division of Christian Education of the National Council of the Churches of Christ in the United States of America. Used by permission. All rights reserved.

For my daughters

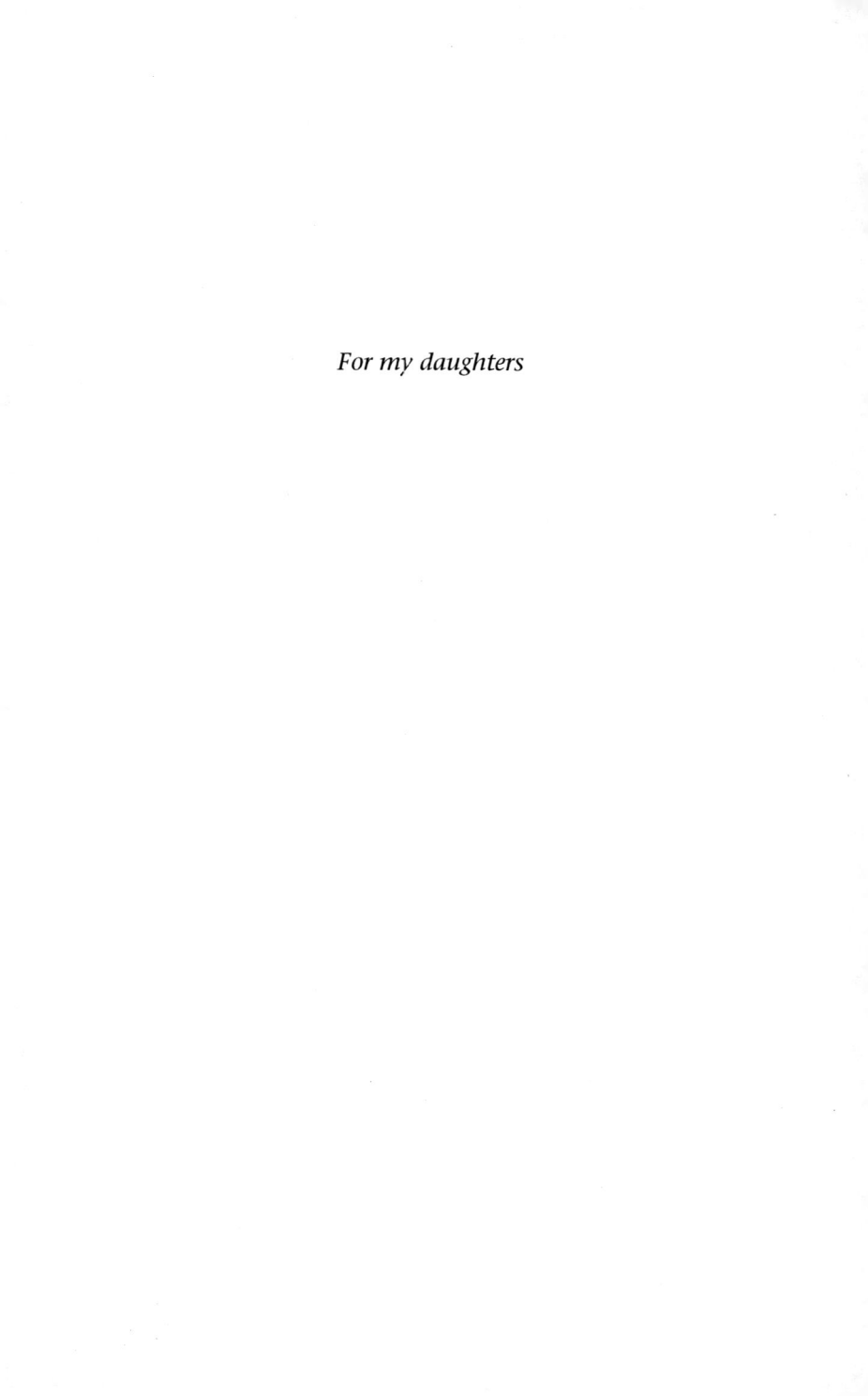

To be a guardian [of the great spiritual work] signifies two things: the study of and practical application of the heritage of the past, and secondly continuous creative effort aiming at the advancement of the work. For the Tradition lives only when it is deepened, elevated, and increased in size. Conservation alone does not suffice at all.

—Valentin Tomberg

Contents

Foreword by Phyllis Tickle | ix

Acknowledgments | xi

Introduction | 1

Dialogues: Becoming Flame | 9

Notes | 53

Afterword | 55

Questions for Study Groups | 57

Bibliography | 59

The Mother and Daughter saw a great ship on the horizon, its sails catching the red and gold of the morning rays.

"I long to be carried by such a glorious ship to the land of my hopes and dreams," wished the Daughter aloud.

"You have been blessed with just such a Ship," said the Mother.

"What is its name?" asked the Daughter.

Her Mother replied: "It is your Soul."

—From *Becoming Flame*

Foreword

THE GENIUS of *Becoming Flame* lies in Anders's singular ability to both occupy and employ the tone and cadence of wisdom literature effectively and without violation to the historical integrity of that genre.

The words and dialogues given us here could just as easily have been those of the Desert Mothers themselves. Certainly the thrust and breadth of Anders's insights are resonant with those of all the wise women of faith who have preceded us.

I cannot imagine either a mother or a daughter who will not be the richer for having read and savored these dialogues. But just as much to the point is the fact that I cannot imagine sons or fathers who will not likewise find themselves to be the richer for having read and savored.

What is here is the eternal feminine in its most sacred presentations, and all people, regardless of gender, yearn to know and be embraced by that hallowed fullness.

This truly is a remarkable piece of work, and it's an honor to be asked to be a part of it.

Phyllis Tickle
The Farm in Lucy
Millington, Tennessee

Acknowledgments

I warmly thank my longtime agent, Tracy Grant, for believing in this "different" approach to wisdom literature, despite its lack of precedent and quiet audacity of voice; for her perseverance, good judgment, and generous spirit of ongoing cooperation in the venture. *Becoming Flame* would not be experiencing this unveiling without her.

Special thanks must also be expressed to Virginia Wagnon, for sharing in its journey; to Phyllis Tickle for caring and encouraging me as it developed; to Diane M. Moore and Victoria Sullivan for priceless support at crucial moments; to KiKi Crombie for enduring friendship; to Sr. Elizabeth Mills for the heart-listening that is praying; and as always, to my husband Bill Keller, who never stopped believing.

Introduction

What is to give light must endure burning.
—Viktor Frankl

It is not for nothing that Wisdom is personified as a woman in the Old Testament, as in Proverbs 8: " . . . *whoever finds me finds life"* (v. 35a; cf Sir. 1:9–10; Wis. of Sol. 7:22).

Sophia compels, she personifies, she *attracts*—as the aspect of God who draws the wise into the sphere of Divine Wisdom. It is an exquisite and arresting image with wide-ranging literary importance. Yet, despite the strength of this tradition in recognizing the feminine nature of wisdom in the world, it is also undeniably evident that women in society have *not* been generally deemed as wise, or to be sought out as purveyors of the essence of truth. Exceptions found in history and literature of the wise crone, the otherworldly seer, and the wise grandmother in traditional tales only serve to underline the rule.

There are reasons for this disconnect. The essentially *feminine nature* of the pursuit of wise living is a concept not easily grasped, and it is largely lost on a world that expects knowledge at its fingertips, statistics to guide its choices, and instant verification of the quantifiable personal profit achieved by its actions.

We often hear of "women's intuition," or feminine accuracy credited with the summing up of character or emotional intent in a given situation. Sir Arthur Conan Doyle includes this insight in one of his Sherlock Holmes novels: "I have seen too much not to know that the impression of a woman may be more valuable than the conclusion of an analytical reasoner." (As though a woman could not be both.)

It is my premise that the overarching value of *woman's way in the world,* and the slower process through which she gains experience, sifts and filters it through her natural stages of development, and eventually finds a confident voice is vastly underrated—and often completely ignored within larger circles of power and influence.

Susan Cahill writes in the Introduction to her anthology *Wise Women:* "Perhaps because it has been women's task throughout history 'to go on believing in life when there was almost no hope,' in the words of Margaret Mead, women have sought and cultivated the goods of the spirit out of a practical need for meaning" (1996, p. xv). Cahill also quotes Elizabeth A. Johnson from her book *She Who Is,* celebrating God as "'relational aliveness,' a masculine/feminine force of mutuality" that implies "open-heartedness and change as signs of the presence of a holy spirit" (p. xvi). Clearly women's equal participation in this dynamic is essential to the visitation of such a spirit.

All of this, I maintain, makes women's essential wisdom all that much more the *"treasure" that is better than gold and choice silver,* to visit again the Bible's Proverbs

(8:19)—because women's wisdom is *not* easily or perfunctorily described or even necessarily *recognized* in the midst of the world's many competing systems and authorities. Like the unseen wind, or breath, spirit blows where it will and engenders *change*—sometimes without visible means. Women's relative invisibility in higher circles of power suggests a quality of mystery and depth of influence not easily grasped.

> It is a rare
> And a high way,
> Which the soul follows,
> Drawing the senses after.
> —Mechthild of Magdeburg

Woman's wisdom is, of course, as particular as an individual woman herself, as only in the context of real-life dilemmas and choices can true wisdom become actualized. The proof of wisdom is in the health, in the largest sense, of the one who is nurtured by it, as any mother knows in her soul.

While general rules can be helpful in evaluating life's values: "Wise conduct is pleasure to a person of understanding" (Prov. 10:23b), women's wisdom acknowledges the ambiguity and fluidity of life's besetting issues and fluctuating situations. And effectively implementing women's wisdom always requires *something more*—an actualized understanding—to come to the fore and literally *bring life* out of chaos. "The mother's service is nearest, readiest and surest," concluded fourteenth-century English mystic Julian of Norwich in her *Showings*. From this insight we can also infer an aspect of God's care for all creation.

Historian Caroline Walker Bynum has observed in her book *Holy Feast and Holy Fast* that "women's symbols express contradiction and opposition less than synthesis and paradox" (1988, p. 289). There is in feminine sensibility a movement toward union rather than disengagement. Yet women's complex, real lives in the physical world make achieving the positive values of synthesis and union difficult. Connection with others in harmony, in the midst of the many challenges of physical existence, is a goal and a vision that can be achieved only through hard-won discipline and clear thinking.

Women's wisdom consists of understanding and application of *appropriateness within a context.* And so I have sought to express something of the flavor of such passing on of wisdom within a mother-daughter question-and-answer mode—a model that does not need to be limited to actual physical mother-daughter relations, but rather serves to embody classic inquiry and interaction in various circumstances between a woman mentor and anyone with ears to hear.

Why a dialogical structure? An alternate translation of the Prologue to the Gospel of John is said to be: "In the beginning was the conversation and the conversation was God . . . and in the fullness of time that conversation entered into our flesh." *Becoming* requires understanding. This is the sort of realization and actualization that women partake of naturally—an accumulation of human experience that has grown in response to specific challenges, a process that we *enflesh.*

Principles of enfleshment and incarnation are not, of course, limited in application only to *women's* lives. However, often in the case of women and their children undergoing the very physical battles of sustenance and survival, stunning victories for good and the truth that result will remain silent and unrecorded, such as experiences of a woman persevering through a difficult labor, holding a burning child lovingly all night until his fever breaks, or embracing love unflinchingly and at great personal cost.

Maternal thinking as a form of wisdom has vast implications, moreover, beyond a mode of rearing and nurturing children. The essence of life-giving wisdom that women may embody has long been marginalized and trivialized. Perhaps it is simply too easy to consider the essential operations of hearth and home as peripheral, rather than as the primary basis for sustaining the essence of life itself.

Yet, quite appropriately, we find many profound "feminine" insights among early Christian mystics, men and women who were "birthing" their faith, and I believe that a recognition of such wisdom is ripe for revitalization. As thirteenth-century German mystic Mechthild of Magdeburg wrote: "Even though we are as a small vessel, yet Thou hast filled it. . . . "

Carol Lee Flinders in her book *Enduring Grace: Living Portraits of Seven Women Mystics*, explains the maternal thinking of philosopher Sara Ruddick: "Ruddick emphasizes that women tell stories to one another out of their daily experience, stories that are meant to strengthen [their] values in themselves and one another. [Women's] visionary writings . . . can be seen as just this—concrete, highly visual, and often quite intimate ways of presenting the spiritual teachings that a learned theologian might treat in a much more abstract manner" (1993, p. 8).

St. Catherine of Siena in the fourteenth century was able simply to assert, "If you are what you should be, you will set the whole world on fire." St. Teresa of Avila famously wrote in *Interior Castle,* "Let us imagine that within us is an extremely rich palace, built entirely of gold and precious stones. . . . " And of women themselves she observed, "All of this imagining is necessary that we may truly understand that within us lies something incomparably more precious than what we see outside ourselves." The Sufi poet Rumi echoes this truth by seeing the visible world as the "microcosm," while for him the true macrocosm is the vast world of the spirit within.

Various world religious traditions through the ages have offered us aspects of wisdom delivered in dialogical forms—many of which continue to inspire modern seekers after deeper truths. We can treasure the profound and evocative legacy of Hasidic dialogue, of a rabbi or holy man debating truth with his disciples. And we revere the Eastern monastic desert tradition, including the dialogues and parables of the Sufi sages and their followers. What I have sought to do in *Becoming Flame* is to employ this conversational form, drawing from my experience as a woman and a mother, and in a similar manner to convey some essentials of feminine collective wisdom—focusing in on the process itself, as wisdom is "kneaded" and "made" like bread.

One trait shared by the various strains of dialogical wisdom is the personal commitment that is required from one's soul in order even to approach the wisdom elicited through the dialogues. And so I title this collection *Becoming Flame:*

"Holy One," a disciple is said to have asked a master within the context of a traditional "school" of learning. "What is the difference between knowledge and wisdom?" It is passed down to us that the Holy One answered: "When you have knowledge, you use a torch to show the way. When you are wise, you become the torch."

Such ultimate self-offering aptly describes the lifegiving way of Jesus (Phil. 2:5–8), to whom the Apostle Paul refers in 1 Corinthians 1:24 as "the wisdom of God." Though this book is not explicitly based on Jesus' wisdom teachings, the principles and the spirit of them inform and permeate my own Christian understanding and application throughout. It could hardly be otherwise.

The pursuit of inner wisdom and the willingness to implement it as much as possible in the world, among all others, is not for the fainthearted. Yet, not to seek wisdom, to plead disinterest, timidity, repugnance, or fear is to walk headlong into the far-worse fires of ignorance and destruction—for oneself and for those one inevitably brings along. If such wisdom can begin within us and find its way through barriers of flesh and skin to accomplish visible transformation of our own and others' lives—it truly is the pearl of great price of which Jesus spoke in Matthew 13:45.

The Dominican mystic Meister Eckhart (c. 1260–1327/8) dwelt in the world of paradoxical wisdom and was considered a heretic in his time—yet he speaks timelessly to all generations and to both genders when he says: "The soul must long for God in order to be set aflame by God's love; but if the soul cannot yet feel this longing, then it must long for the longing. To long for the longing is also from God."

And so, if the word "wisdom" is like a spark to your soul, a glimpse of light flickering on an unreached shore, a flash above the horizon that at least compels you to move in the direction of its promised heat and light, then you may be in the early stages of desiring, along with saints and awakened ones through the ages, the privilege and the sacrifice of *Becoming Flame*.

Isabel Anders
Everafter Cottage
Sewanee, Tennessee

Hearthside Wisdom

The Daughter asked: "How do you spin all day, and see so little for your effort, and keep from discouragement?"

The Mother answered: "See this little square of texture and design? It is enough to wrap the universe in comfort and warmth."

The Daughter was perplexed. "How can this be?"

The Mother replied: "Even a few inches of loving intent can spread to span continents. Ask a ray of sun."

⚭

The Daughter wondered that the Mother could spend so much time lovingly tending the fire, stirring the soup, and baking the bread.

"Do you not tire of such mundane tasks?"

"This substance," the Mother explained, breaking bread, "makes possible the 'alchemy' of life. Through it the roughness of grain is transformed into the fine constituents of our Being. . . . How can this be called mundane?"

The Daughter asked, "How does one find the Truth amid the myriad choices of every day's confusion?"

"See the ball of tangled threads at my feet?" asked the Mother. "Many colors are bound together into a knot of complexity. But take the end of any one string, and follow it to its beginning, and you will by your effort reach the Center."

After a morning of washing and mending, making beds and sweeping cobwebs from dark corners of the house, the Daughter paused to ask: "We repeat the same movements, do the same work over and over, week after week, year after year. When will we ever be *done?*"

The Mother paused to take in her child's weariness of tone and answered her: "Choosing order over chaos begins in quiet movements and deliberate acts. Even as we bend and reach we are serving Beauty. It is enough to be its slaves on some days."

"On cleaning day!" the Daughter agreed, and went back to work.

When the pantry shelves began to appear empty, and more supplies were needed to last the week, the Daughter offered to go to market for the family's needs.

"Why is it that we shrink from Emptiness—barren fields, dry wastes, depleted cupboards, and winter's silences?" she pondered aloud.

Her Mother paused and replied, "Life's spaces seem to demand something of us in human response; and emptiness evokes doubts in us that we can successfully meet a need, or bring back growth. Spaces are as much symbols as objects are, and silences speak if we are able to listen . . . "

"I will be back from the market soon," the Daughter assured her Mother, "and we will spread the table with our Answer."

※

The next morning was fair and cloudless, and the Daughter opened her window and exulted in the new day dawning.

"Today I feel I could run a race without touching the ground!" she shouted to her parents.

"If you do," said her Mother, "it will be because you learned that technique from your Heart."

The Flame of Life

The Daughter dreamed of rings of fire, flame chasing flame in endless circles of dazzling light. The dance of their movement before her eyes seemed to tease her into a delirium of joy.

"Why do I see sights and hear sounds in my dreams that *cannot be* when I wake?" she asked her Mother.

"What eyes have not seen and ears have not heard *are* exactly what awaits us. Not yet simply means not yet," her Mother admonished.

⊗

The Daughter knew that, as she grew, her days in her Mother's presence were dwindling down. She sensed that she must gather Wisdom as she was able before their eventual separation.

"What is the purpose of your life, Mother?" she asked one day.

"Why is a grain of sand? What holds the stars? Where is tomorrow? If I knew the answers to these questions, the purpose of my own life would be a mere footnote to be read sometime, with amusement, at leisure."

When the candle by her bedside guttered and died out, the Daughter watched the smoke rise from its darkened wick.

"Are you going to sleep now?" her Mother asked from the other room.

"Sometimes the darkness decides for me," she answered. "But it is because I do not yet know how to rekindle my own flame."

"Let the days and the nights teach you, Child, it is the only way," her Mother assured her.

※

The Daughter feared the dark and wished not to be alone, away from her parents in the cold, inhospitable world.

"Do not fear," said the Mother. "You are not a bruised reed or a flickering wick. The flame that burns within you is designed to withstand all weathers. Only trust."

"But I do not feel its light, its warmth, at all moments," the Daughter protested. "Sometimes it seems extinguished and cold."

Her Mother answered: "Those are the moments at which it burns brightest."

The Flame of Life

The Mother spent all day in the fields of harvest while the Daughter tended the fire and prepared the family's evening meal.

When the Mother returned to the house, the fire had gone out and darkness had leaked into the dwelling.

"Why did you allow the fire to die down?" the Mother asked.

"The bread was baked, the meal complete," the Daughter explained.

"But," her Mother said kindly, "fire is more than its function, just as your life is more than your tasks. At day's end we take heart in seeing each other's faces around a well-lit table. This is a picture of Life at the end of all Time."

Moonscapes

The slender new moon outside the Daughter's window seemed nearly transparent—as though she could see the Other World through its translucent gauze. "What will my destiny be?" she implored of her Mother.

"You will be one who asks the Bigger Questions—*see*—this Truth is unfolding even as you ask," her Mother pointed out.

※

The Daughter could not sleep. The half-light of the Moon crept into her room and lay heavy on her closed eyelids. Her own thoughts filled her to the brim with wakefulness and struggle.

"What is the matter with me, Mother?" she asked the next morning after her fitful night.

"Nights are not always meant for sleep," her Mother reminded her. "Pay attention to the moment, awake or asleep, and it will fill your need to Be as you are in that instant."

"But what if I do not sleep tonight as well?" she asked, troubled.

"The attention of your Soul will wax and wane like the Moon itself," her Mother assured her. "Do not disdain one state or the other. To experience both is what is meant by Fullness of Being."

The Daughter asked the Mother: "You have lived through many moons. Is there any day in which you have *not* felt the rush of Time, the incompleteness of life, the unbearable smallness of our part in the great Universe?"

"Yes," said the Mother.

"What day is that?" the Daughter inquired.

"Tomorrow," her Mother answered serenely.

※

The Mother remembered when she had cradled her Daughter in her arms, an infant of possibility and delight. Now the Daughter stood full to her own height and carried burdens beyond her own capacity.

"Tell me of my early days," the Daughter implored. "Was I always gazing at the moon, looking for Something Else?"

"Yes," remembered the Mother. "And thus the Child extends the boundaries of the Mother from the first day of its life. This is a part of what is meant by Immortality."

Under the Sun

"Some days I think I know the Truth and feel I am guided from Above. But at other times I feel lost and confused, as too many possibilities flare out on either side of me," said the Daughter.

"Just as the sun is too powerful to look upon with naked eyes, yet we can observe it safely reflected in a stream of water," answered her Mother, "so the Truth itself must be filtered into our lives through particular events and moments. Do not ask for more, but garner Truth as eagerly as you gather blossoms from the meadow—abundantly and joyously."

⁂

"See the cat lying in the sun?" the Daughter pointed out to her Mother. "How does it find the time to bask at its leisure every day?"

"It does not *find* the time," counseled the Mother. "By its very Being it *creates* Time."[1]

The Daughter was discouraged. She had failed to spin the daily quota of fine threads, and the small result of her efforts lay limply in her lap.

"What is the matter?" the Mother asked. "Have you lost sight of how each day's effort forms an integral part of the Whole?"

"But what if I cannot complete the work?" the Daughter asked.

"That is the Question that lies at the heart of every moment, and it is also the power that sustains the work at every juncture. Yet, in a paradox, it is only by setting the Question aside and attending to the moment that the Question comes within the realm of being answered."

※

The bright afternoon stream of the winter sun shone directly, hitting the eyes of Mother and Daughter as they sat by the window and shared a moment of repose.

"The sun is so bright that I see less rather than more in its light," the Daughter said, shielding her eyes.

"On these afternoons we seem to have more of the sun than we can accommodate—though for a shorter time, as it sinks in but a few hours," her Mother agreed. "It is like Youth in its glory—like your own shining countenance!" she observed. "Enjoy it while it shines on you."

The Mother and Daughter saw a great ship on the horizon, its sails catching the red and gold of the morning rays.

"I long to be carried by such a glorious ship to the land of my hopes and dreams," wished the Daughter aloud.

"You have been blessed with just such a Ship," said the Mother.

"What is its name?" asked the Daughter.

Her Mother replied: "It is your Soul."

The Narrow Path

"Take down this Book," said the Mother to the Daughter. "In it you will find a goodly measure of what my days of living can convey to you in words. It is Wisdom from the soul, and it will sustain you when I am gone."

"But what it teaches is so *simple*," the Daughter protested: "'Love God first, and others as yourself, and all shall be well.'"

"Yes," admitted the Mother. "But the reading and the knowing of this Truth are like the path toward a narrow gate; they serve to mark that you are on the right Way. It is the *understanding* and the *living* of this Truth—entering the gate—that requires *all you can give and Be,* forevermore."

※

"Sometimes it seems so limiting to be a woman, to be smaller with a quieter voice, and to be treated as invisible in certain circles simply because of this," the Daughter reflected.

Her Mother reminded her, "To be embodied at all is to know limitation for a purpose—male or female—yet there is much room for variety and difference even within one gender's path. You, by your choices, by your actions, expand what it means to be not only a woman, but a particular soul."

The Mother declared an end to work for the day and called her Daughter simply to sit on the front porch by her side, enjoying the twilight.

"But what of the work yet undone?" the Daughter inquired. "Will not tomorrow's demands press us unbearably if we stop now?"

Her Mother replied: "There will always be doubt and uncertainty while we are in Time. But such concerns must not keep us from the Living that all our tasks are meant to serve: the Being Together."

※

The Daughter recounted, "When I was on the path today, there were large stones blocking my way. I feared I could go no farther."

The Mother asked, "Were there no others who could help?"

"No," the Daughter told her. "I was alone, and I feared the rocks at my feet would prevent me from completing my Task."

"But you are mistaken," said her Mother. "Rather than being barriers, the stones *were* your task."

"What lies beyond the sky?" asked the Daughter playfully. "Those clouds look for all the world like another shore."

"Perhaps. But the edge of your next experience is also an unexplored shore," her Mother said. "You may step onto a new plane of Being while moving about on the ground beneath your feet."

The Garden of Life

The Daughter loved to hear stories of her own growth into young womanhood. "Yet, my life is still such a small entity in the vast Universe," she mused to her Mother, as they gazed together at the stars. "How can I be important enough to claim a Future and know Meaning?"

"If you want to know the Universe," advised her Mother, "remember that *you* are a small portion of it yourself, with inner receptors that can serve to transform your Soul into a beacon of lights and marvels. If you look within *as well as* Above you will find the secret of Being that holds the worlds together. It goes by the name of 'Love.'"

"Do all green things on earth, all birds and creatures truly 'Bless the Lord' by their Being, as we sing of in our worship?" asked the Daughter.

"We affirm it to be so, despite our limited understanding." Her mother paused, then continued: "But even in our lack of full comprehension, *let us too praise* with the hearts and tongues that we as humans have been given!"[2]

The small fig tree that the Daughter had planted seemed to be losing in its struggle to grow and thrive. She held one of its branches sadly in one hand and asked aloud, "How did I fail it?"

Her Mother replied, "Not all life is meant to endure—conditions were too harsh, the soil did not support it—you are not to blame."

"But I feel sad anyway," the Daughter replied. "I identify with its diminishment."

"Then the fig tree has already taught you something that a thriving plant could not," her Mother surmised.

The Daughter sat shelling beans, her hands agile and active, culling the usable pulp from the discarded ends. A large bowl of the green pods, brimming crisp and discrete, sat next to her on the step.

"What should I do with these useless ends?" she asked her Mother, who walked by carrying a hoe.

"Return them to the garden, Daughter. There they will join with the earth to be remade and re-harvested as usable food."

"Will we, too, receive a second chance at Life?"

"*All that is* may spring into new Life. Just as everything is made of one Substance, so, too, our lives are really *one* thing. Only we ourselves imagine divisions of 'this life' or 'that life.' Life truly is indivisible."

The Daughter noted how the daffodils appeared within a certain week, early in Spring, springing up along the walkway to their front door, as though on cue each year.

"These are perennials," explained her Mother. "They do not need to wait for another planting to make their appearance and grace the Earth with their beauty and cheer."

"How do the flowers know when they are once again called to bloom?" asked the Daughter.

"They are following the Pattern," explained her Mother. "The seed that dies within the Earth remembers its former glory, its magnificent template of design. The individual seed only awaits its moment to reappear and flower in its day."

"I look forward to their springing forth every year!" the Daughter cried with delight.

"Yes," said the Mother. "And remember that your own joy flows from the same Energy that sends its life through the green stem, into the yellow flute."

"I, too, flower in that knowledge," said the Daughter, laughing with understanding.

The Daughter asked her Mother: "Why must we rake the garden and remove the stones, spread the mulch, dig proper holes, and water and tend our plantings with such care?"

The Mother pointed out, "We labor continually against the chaos that would despoil Earth if we did not do our part. It would not take long for the garden to be ravaged and ruined without our efforts. All systems wind down, without an input of appropriate Energy."

"Then we are very *important,* are we not? By our work we tame and mold the lower elements."

"Ah, but therein lies the greatest mystery of Being," admitted her Mother. "Yes, we are good Stewards, and these labors help to define our worth. But we must see ourselves always as 'in-betweens,' for even greater, unseen Energies at higher levels oversee our human work. There is never room for pride."

Patterns of Wisdom

The Mother and Daughter were gathering mountain stone with which the Father intended to build a small wall around the garden. Together they dug out and lifted the earthen-colored shapes that they knew he would somehow fit together to create an artful barrier in its place.

"Father will be pleased at the treasures we have uncovered," the Daughter mused.

"And we too are building even as we gather, for the plans and the completion are already foretold in the mute presence of the stones themselves," her Mother observed.

※

Clouds hung just above the distant mountain range, making the heights appear hazily extended, unreachable, sublime.

"Look how the mountain has grown!" exclaimed the Daughter playfully.

"Just so," said her Mother, "our thoughts and dreams extend to planes beyond our reach today. But what our inner eye can envision and our heart desire will, *all of it,* add height and depth to our real, unfolding Future, much as the clouds 'expand' the mountains."

"But how are we to hold all that our dreams contain, along with the promise of the far vistas—all in a solitary lifetime?" the Daughter wondered.

"Do not fear. Through it all, our inner world expands to receive the last drop from the eternal river that will be given us in our final breath. This expansion is what it means to be alive," the Mother replied.

※

"How will I know, when I reach a crossroads," the Daughter asked, concerned, "which direction to take?"

"The patterns of all your choices to this point—and their consequences—will echo in your inner senses," assured the Mother. "You will 'see' what cannot be scratched on a fingerpost or written in the sand. *You will know the Way to go*—you will embrace it with your heart."[3]

"Your Soul," said the Mother, "calls to you in ways that are mirrored in the natural world: At times it implores with the frisky eagerness of a squirrel; at others it shares the lassitude of a hibernating bear. Each mood and stance will teach you something of yourself as you face the world."

"Why do I feel one way toward my Destiny now, and the next day another?" asked the Daughter, perplexed.

"The Way itself is more of a labyrinth than a direct path," her Mother assured her. "You will learn more from the arcs and curves and unexpected byways than from the straight lines of your journey."

"What does it mean to be human, to be a woman or a man?" the Daughter asked plainly.

"Your body itself is a meeting place, a living crossroads between the smallest particles of Being and the elements that make up the farthest galaxies," her Mother responded. "Though your cells are in constant interchange with the stuff of the Universe—yet *you* define in your body *what it is to be human* as you perpetuate the Pattern. What is more, you can recognize this humanness in another by mere encounter. This realization forms the essence of mutual respect."

"There is someone at the door," the Daughter called to her Mother and Father. "How can I ever know if it is safe to open up—as there is much evil walking the road?"

"The virtue of caution is meant to be a part of mature wisdom. But overvigilance must not be allowed to paralyze the Soul—or the same door that shuts out danger may serve to bar the entrance of fulfillment and ecstasy as well. . . . " The Mother smiled and glanced out the window. "Now, let us welcome together our guests who have arrived early!"

※

"Is there truly a Plan," asked the Daughter, "that can guide me in every decision and assure me that I am choosing rightly?"

"You must bring your whole self to that question. Then, at the point where your deepest conviction intersects the line of present opportunity, you will be shown the Way. That is all we can ask for on this Earth," said her Mother.

Breath of Life

The Daughter said, "All of our work is so material, kneading dough, plowing the garden, tending the fires without and within. . . . It is difficult to believe in the Unseen that surrounds us, even on nights crowned by burning lights in the heavens."

"Yes, it is always difficult to believe in the Unseen. But your own breath teaches you that there are interim states between spirit and matter. The elements that are not seen: the wind, your breath, the Spirit that moves among us, show themselves only in their effects. Therefore, which is more real? The Sources or their effects?"

"I am supposed to ask the questions!" protested the Daughter teasingly.

⚭

"If we are made of light and air, and dubious 'matter,' why do we not float away? Where is this 'Life' we have that is so precious, though unseen?" the Daughter pondered aloud.

"You do not expect a fish to drown in water, nor birds to be rejected by the sky. Just so, we are fitted for our habitat here, with skins to protect our inner organs and eyes to perceive both outer and inner realities. Never neglect one for the other," the Mother advised.

"Are we truly 'feathers on the breath of God' as Hildegard[4] taught? Have we no will of our own?" the Daughter asked.

"There are two answers," the Mother explained deliberately. "In the moment we *can* exercise a choice. But all that has led to that choice has been painstakingly constructed through the building up of our true Selves. If we cannot see God's hand in that process and give thanks, we will feel truly alone in the Universe."

"I long to form the words that are on the tip of my tongue when I awake, but they dissolve always in the morning air," lamented the Daughter. "I want to say to myself: *'This is the meaning of Life.'*"

"How can one find the way to where Souls are distributed? Can you place an order for your next breath? Who has the wisdom to corral the clouds? When the dance floor is full of whirling figures, can you distinguish the dancers from the Dance?"

"Is there no answer then?"

"Just keep dancing," her Mother assured her lovingly.

Breath of Life 41

"How will I know what to look for in my Journey?" the Daughter asked doubtfully.

"As Heraclitus, the 'weeping philosopher,' put it: *'If we do not expect the unexpected we will never find it,'*" her Mother admonished.

※

"Do plants breathe?" the Daughter queried.

"They breathe out exactly what we ourselves need to survive on this Planet."

"How thoughtful of the Creator[5] to give us each other."

"And to give you to me," said the Mother, tightly hugging her Daughter.

※

"When we speak of 'the Spirit,' how do we know it is the one of God?" worried the Daughter.

"We are always to 'test the spirits' we discern in our lives, and then to follow after Truth by observing in which direction they have moved us."

Earthen Treasure

"My body is subject to sudden moods and changes each month," the Daughter reflected. "How have you managed to live through decades of Womanhood with these impediments?"

"When my body has cried 'Limitation!' I have learned to unfold the wings that are buried in my Heart and to soar within its inner depth," confessed the Mother.

⚭

"Is woman but a vessel, to bear her lot and carry forth life for others?"

"Every valued substance must be carried to be taken toward its Destiny. You are a vessel greatly prized, and you yourself can choose to convey either the weakest water or the choicest wine. The shape of your Soul *does* partake of receptivity, and this Truth is meant to contribute to your fulfillment on Earth," said the Mother.

The Daughter held a hinged scallop shell in her hand. "Often I feel that my heart is closed, like this shell," she revealed. "Who will come to open it?"

"You are a priceless jewel and flower of my life," the Mother told her Daughter. "All creatures are designed to sing in their own time. It is in the *waiting for love* that true Love gains strength, and in time its music swells to fill the Heart."

⁂

"As Sophocles wrote in the *Phaedra,* 'Children are the anchors that hold a mother to Life.' You are my investment in the future of the world . . . my own precious dividend," the Mother said.

"Then let me pay for my part in coinage of Love," the Daughter said, hugging her Mother.

Woman and Man

"From where does true Love come, and how will I know it when it appears?"

"Remember the lessons of the Word, the garden, the seasons, and the night sky—and gather all the wisdom from your old loves of parents and pets, friends and mentors. Deep in the center of that rich bouquet lies the answer."

※

"How do you and Father continue loving, through so many years of difficulty, toil and disappointments?" the Daughter asked.

"The dawning of love is like the morning, but its trajectory will take you through the lean years and the bleak and barren days," the Mother admitted. "Nevertheless, you hold onto Love for dear Life—for your own Destiny is defined in its folds."[6]

"Why does Father hold a different place in the scheme of Love? He is a planter and a builder, a merchant and a strong presence in the marketplace. His masculine voice and strength hold others to attention," the Daughter observed.

"Everything, every gift is given in a certain degree. I too have had my times to speak decisively and be heard. And he has learned to listen," the Mother replied.

"How does marriage free as well as bind lovers?" the Daughter asked wonderingly.

"To me, freedom is to know that my love is lovingly returned," her Mother said simply.

"What will sustain me most in the years and decades of a committed love?" the Daughter wondered.

Her Mother answered without hesitation: "Always seek, as much as you are able, to be the Christ to each other."

The Far Shore

"Is there a Place beyond this one where all of our half-understandings find completion? I long for it now, every day," admitted the Daughter.

"To look for a 'Place' called Paradise is to talk in children's sing-song. And yet, we are all still children, even I!" The Mother smiled.

"Then what are we to expect of our Future?"

"The winged soul, like the butterfly, finds the Garden that suits its nature. Live the Truth and desire God, and heaven will unfold before your eyes."

"How can I begin to travel 'There'?"

"Sincere desire for the Eternal is the beginning of wisdom. You are already on the Path, my Daughter."

"But it will take too long, perhaps my whole lifetime. What if I forget to be on the Way and lose sight of the goal?"

"In this Vale of Soulmaking, even our forgetfulness is beaten into the mix, like dry flour that is folded into the oil and cream, so that no trace of doubt or weakness is allowed to spoil the result."

The Far Shore 49

"Mother, you have been a mirror to me of things Unseen, until my desire for Truth grows into a hunger to know *now*."

"Let my life then be more of a *spyglass* through which you may view *your* unique Path and Destiny. Though I have lived longer than you, still we are like two infants in the womb debating the parameters of the world outside!"

"But I so need a guide."

"If my life serves to point you toward the True Horizon, that is all a fellow-traveler can offer."

※

The day was spent, and a pink and gold sunset promised the opening up of another World beyond the sea. Even the clouds seemed to beckon to a far Country not unlike their own—only gloriously lit with light from an unseen Source.

"Can we travel there—now?" asked the Daughter, pointing playfully.

"After you," said her Mother, laughing and holding out an arm. "Did not the great Philo[7] say that if one has experienced the wisdom that can only be heard from oneself, learned from oneself, and created from oneself—she does not merely participate in laughter: she becomes laughter itself?"

Coda

The Daughter raced home from the field on her coming-of-age birthday to find a well-lit room full of celebration and warmth. There her Mother and her Father sat, surrounded by gifts chosen to thrill her heart. They hugged and kissed her, showering exclamations and wishes beyond all reason, sprinkled upon her like holy water to grace her future.

"How you spoil and honor me, when all I have done is grown another year older!" the Daughter protested teasingly.

"We celebrate the miracle of Life in you, your emergence in strength and particularity, against all the odds," said her Mother.

Added her Father: "And to *the Three in One:* Glory and praise evermore! Truly this is the gate of heaven, and the way of blessing."

"And now let us cut the cake!" the Daughter responded with glee.

What no eye has seen, nor ear heard, nor the human heart conceived, what God has prepared for those who love him.
—1 Corinthians 2:9

"When the soul is plunged in the fire of divine love, like iron, it first loses its blackness, and then growing to white heat it becomes like unto the fire itself. And lastly, it grows liquid, and, losing its nature, is transmuted into an utterly different quality of being. And as the difference between iron that is cold and iron that is hot, so is the difference between soul and soul, between the tepid soul and the soul made incandescent by divine love."
—Richard of St. Victor

"Love one another."
—Jesus

Notes

1. St. Augustine believed that since God exists in a timeless eternity, it is only through created beings that the concept of time becomes meaningful, as they are able to have a past, present, and future.

2. Abba Hyperichius [fourth-century monk and desert father] said, "Praise God continually with spiritual hymns and always remain in meditation and in this way you will be able to bear the burden of the temptations that come upon you. A traveler who is carrying a heavy load pauses from time to time and draws in deep breaths; it makes the journey easier and the burden lighter."

3. "The early church fathers used to speak of a pathway of perception they called *epinoia,* which meant knowing through intuition and direct revelation, not through the linear and didactic *dianoia* of logic and doctrine and dogma." —Quotation from Cynthia Bourgeault in *The Wisdom Jesus* (Boston and London: Shambhala, 2008), p. 19.

4 Hildegard of Bingen (1098–1179): "All the arts serving human desires and needs are derived from the breath that God sent into the human body."

5 "The word creation is one of the great symbol-words describing the relation of God to the Universe"

   —Quotation from Paul Tillich, source unknown.

6 Amma Syncletica [fourth-century desert mother] said, "In the beginning there are a great many battles and a good deal of suffering for those who are advancing towards God and, afterwards, ineffable joy. It is like those who wish to light a fire. At first they are choked with smoke and cry, until they obtain what they seek. As it is written, 'Our God is a consuming fire' (Heb 12:29); so we also must kindle the divine fire in ourselves through tears and hard work."

7 Philo of Alexandria (c. 20 BC–c. 50 AD) was a Hellenistic Jewish philosopher who may have influenced the Apostle Paul and other New Testament writers.

Afterword

Open your eyes to phenomena.

Attune your ears to outer and inner voices that speak fulfillment.

Allow your heart to encompass the worlds that overlap your given experience.

The language and the process of becoming flame are drawn from a feminine wisdom that includes three basic components: a healthy receptivity to what is; an openness to fullness of being; and active employment of "practical love."

Barbara J. Monda writes in her "revisioning" of the Psalms, *Rejoice, Beloved Woman* (2004):

> *Happy are you who trust in the counsel of wise women.*
>
> *They guide you to a right heart. . . .*

> *The holy among you appear as any other. Their counsel, however, comes from truth aligned to all there is; they exaggerate nothing.*
>
> *It is by the gift that the giver is known. See what you have when a woman leaves your presence; are you empty or connected to goodness?*[1] (from Psalm 1).

The language of a woman's wisdom will be drawn from her daily life and activities, her inner vision and work, and her unique expression of these laws of life as they are worked out in exquisite particularity in time and space.

Breathe. Live. Love.

What you are will shine out like "shook foil,"[2] in a life naturally and gradually becoming flame.
—IA

---

1. Used by permission.
2. Phrase from Gerard Manley Hopkins' poem "God's Grandeur."

Questions for Study Groups

1. What women in your life have especially taught you the ways of wisdom that work in day-to-day living?

2. How does a woman's inherent receptivity influence her choices and responses to the events of her life? Is receptivity a strictly feminine trait?

3. What images drawn from natural phenomena and earthly sources are most resonant in your own life? What have you been taught through working with such natural substances as bread, or clay, or water? What have you learned through adjusting the parameters of your life over time? What wisdom has come to you in caring for your own and others' bodies?

4. How can wisdom be passed on from one person to another, and one generation to another? How may women's experience of physical birth and infant nurturing contribute to this understanding? How does caring for the needy and the aging relate to this natural feminine connectedness to others?

5. What are the pitfalls of claiming wisdom as one's own? How does humility fit into a life of feminine wisdom?

6. What does "fullness of being" mean in your life? How do one's beliefs become part of one's being? How have you experienced this through the decades of your life so far?

7. What are the characteristics of "practical love," and how does it play out in a woman's life? (Is it any different from such love in a man's experience and life?) What do you think men could learn from women's style of loving?

8. What do you think it means to "become flame" through the various stages of life: as a daughter, a mother, a wife, a worker, and an older wisdom figure? What other images describe the phases and the end result of wisdom permeating a feminine person?

9. Flame consumes but is not itself diminished. How does this principle relate to the spiritual life, or the life within? How are the active, involved aspects of your life intertwined with and supported by times of solitude and inner development?

10. What have you learned from the process of shining for the benefit of God and others rather than for your own glory? How does one *become flame* and enable others to become flame?

Bibliography

Bourgeault, Cynthia. *The Wisdom Jesus*. Boston & London: Shambhala, 2008.

Bynum, Caroline Walker. *Holy Feast and Holy Fast: The Religious Significance of Food to Medieval Women*. Berkeley: University of California Press, 1988.

Cahill, Susan. *Wise Women*. NY: W. W. Norton & Company, 1996.

Flinders, Carol Lee. *Enduring Grace: Living Portraits of Seven Women Mystics*. San Francisco: HarperSanFrancisco, 1993.

Ford-Grabowsky, Mary. *Sacred Voices: Essential Women's Wisdom Through the Ages*. San Francisco: HarperSanFrancisco, 2002.

Monda, Barbara J. *Rejoice, Beloved Woman*. Notre Dame, IN: Sorin Books, 2004.